CROOKED
SPEECH

Also by Sid Gold

Working Vocabulary
The Year of the Dog Throwers
Good With Oranges

Crooked Speech

Poems
Sid Gold

Pond Road Press
Washington, D.C.
North Truro, Mass.

Book design and layout: Patric Pepper
Cover painting: Sid Gold, *Red Desert*, 20" x 16", acrylic
Author photograph: Jessica Lynn Dotson

ISBN: 978-0-9719741-9-7
Library of Congress Control Number: 2018935171

Acknowledgments:
Many thanks to the editors of the print and online magazines, journals
and anthologies where the following poems previously appeared.

Backbone Mountain Review: "Big Dogs," "Locusts," "Old Europe,"
"Punchline," "Roosters," "The Blues," "The Mail," "The Shed,"
"The Word" and "Vendors"
The Broadkill Review: "Dusk," "Little Else," "Lew the Barber,"
"Roadside," "Said," "Season of the Rat," "Storm Warming," "The Crown"
and "The Healer"
Fledgling Rag: "Seawalls" and "Three Wreaths"
Flock: "Chimney" and "Hawk"
Freestate Review: "Crocodile"
Gargoyle: "Cat," "Crawl," "Dream," "Mine," "Noon," "Point," "Stranger"
and "Three"
Innisfree Poetry Journal: "The Knack"
Junction: "Tongues"
Loch Raven Review: "Dog Tags," "The Runners" and "Twins"

Pond Road Press
Mary Ann Larkin and Patric Pepper
221 Channing Street NE
Washington, DC 20002
pepperlarkin@juno.com

Available through Amazon.com and other online
booksellers, and through Pond Road Press.

Contents

The Table

III.

IV.

CROOKED
SPEECH

The Table

My parents, unamicably divorced
since my childhood, are sitting in a diner
waiting upon my arrival. This is the West Side,
just east of Broadway, as my mother
much prefers that my father come to her.

They've agreed not to argue
yet my mother, always suspicious
of my father's still youthful appearance,
has a few sticking points on her mind

& my father, recalling years & years
of relationships fated to fail from the get-go,
tries to decide how many compliments
directed toward my mother will be quite enough.

I enter directly, a bit hurried & apprehensive
but gladdened to see them sitting quietly
& making a show of relative concord.
I, of course, am the sole rationale
for this dinner, my life, that is; my comings
& goings, my present, my future.

Understand I lived almost always
with my mother, so she claims special knowledge
while my father, eyeing the high road, offers
You did a great job, Judy, all those years.
By now, you should know, the waitress is waiting,
the coffee is before us, the table is set.

I.

Space

In Currier & Ives prints, rural life is always depicted as idyllic. The
Dadaists disdained the past as well as the present. Call me a muffin,
dared Camille. I won't care. Ernst, too, was seduced by beauty.
Thebes lay in the central plain of Boetia. Hunter-Gatherers divided
the world into edible & inedible. Abrasive or adhesive? Distant or
distinct? I whirl in the void. Philby possessed an inordinate capacity
for deception. If you can't draw anything else, draw your shoes.
Hallaj was executed by edict of the Caliph in 922. Unsought goes
undetected. No member of a clan will consume its totem animal.
Anyone can experience an epileptic seizure. Faulkner's ideas about
Black-White relations require a careful & objective analysis. Not
haste, but hoist. Not tangerine, but tangent. At the simplest level,
tribal drumming serves as an acoustic fence. The white flowers of
the coca plant resemble tiny apple blossoms. Nevertheless, those
gerbils were imported from Mongolia. Tradition demands that
strangers be fed as soon as they arrive. A spoiler helps vehicles grip
the road at high speeds. All ungulates have hooves. Sleep out in a
hollow log. The only nourishment he knew was grief. Che's parents
encouraged their children to become free thinkers. Out along the
road, the ripe mallow & the wild oat rustle in the wind. A sinister
dawn reddens the sea. Papercut jelly—my favorite!, exclaimed
Irene. That quiet space you left behind.

Dusk

for Mary Ann Larkin

At dusk you might sit
on the front step tossing pebbles
into the darkening air
until there are none at hand.
Across the street, porch lights
brighten one after the other.

The past is a quick reminder
you slip into your pocket.

Crocodile

Sharrock began each morning with a small fix of Coltrane. Byzantine art usually depicts the Magi as wearing Persian garb. Is Todd disappointed? Believe me, he's disappointed. Skilled hurt dancing requires a certain agility. Half-truths motivate the narrative. Grunt or grant? Corset or closet? I'd rather drink muddy water. Heresy is distinct from both blasphemy & apostasy. The ancient Egyptians kept no standing armies. Walk with awareness. Walk through an orchard of stars. To Snake Creek, a century later, I came. In 1835, Mexico placed a bounty on Apache scalps. Psilocybin is present in some 40 species of mushrooms. Ketchup, my darling, you've returned. The Mingus that I knew. Not sink, but zinc. Not pavement, but payment. May I speak the truth to Persea? We can't all be super-imposed, explained the Captain. The ribbed vault is the third Gothic innovation. Aikenhead denied the doctrine of the Trinity. Aye, by all minerals are we mocked. This butcher must be stopped. Voyage or voyeur? Pasture or posture? Odalisque was a Turkish term used to designate the sultan's handmaiden. Playing badminton in the rain. Trumbauer's sound was almost devoid of vibrato. New pan dry spurn view. We, too, belong to the world & it is spread before our eyes. Ask the dangling spider why it takes so long. Three days I lay on the mountain, heart open. Those tall oaks wear their years like ballroom gowns. Ah, that lean & crocodile look.

Testing

Stafford, after a visit
to a former bomb testing site,
wrote about a lizard which,
having sensed something momentous
was about to occur, tensed
like a hair trigger just before detonation.

Meanwhile the sky,
as blue as any of us
envision it, looked on impassively,
keeping its distance, as always,
from human concerns.

We might say detonation was horrible.
We might say it was an *unfortunate necessity*.
We might say nothing at all.

Regardless, most of us will take
a moment or so in choosing our words,
hoping whatever we say, or don't,
will land with the impact we intend.

Not as much as any bomb,
atomic or otherwise, you understand,
but something like that, figuratively speaking.

Cockatoo

By the time Cleopatra was 20, she had been driven out of Egypt by her brother's armies. Morton's rhythmic conception was derived mainly from ragtime. To this the white-armed goddess made no demur. Clever or cleaver? Belt or bolt? Anderson was charged with merely re-hashing Freud's insights. No law denied promiscuous use of concubine or bride. Is that what you really believe?, growled Leland. That change is going to come? Churn doubt just jars. Paul III ruled that the Incas were human beings & should be converted. The Creoles of Color were the descendants of French & Spanish colonials and their slaves. We are blind & we live out our blind lives in blindness. The unexpected youthful stranger bumming toward your door. Not hold, but clinch. Not think, but blink. To date, more than 300 species of dinosaur have been identified. Yet friends take tea together. Someone like Jeanine could not exist in nature, she said with all seriousness. Two separate jobs awaited King Oliver when he first arrived in Chicago. Fantasy demands something extra of us. Thus the old man used the experience of long-ago campaigns to inspire his troops. It's work, I tell you. Hard, exacting work. Young switched from baritone to tenor while playing with The Bostonians. Their monument sticks like a fishbone in the throat of the city. This is for the poor shepherds in our midst. Under my window-ledge the waters race. Store away from heat or open flames. Now nothing can stop him in his mad career. The green freedom of the cockatoo upon a rug.

The Russian Novel

There is the constant threat
of war but speaking perfect French
always takes precedence.

All my lovers
are scandalously unfaithful
& leave me for military officers
only to come running back
when they learn they are pregnant.

No one understands commerce,
cost accounting, ways or means.

Those peasants
who do not doff their hats
when our carriages pass
are left to starve.

Our tutors, Gallic widows
with limited incomes, refuse
to divulge who freed the serfs.
Much of Rome burned long ago,
they teach, but was soon re-built.

Winter commands an army of its own.

A thousand miles west, Franz Kafka—
a shy, tubercular Jew—scribbles incessantly
in a language no one else understands.
Destroy these pages when I'm gone,
he pleads in a Czech-accented German.

Stars

The Rajput code of chivalry demanded mass suicide if no hope of victory remained. Renoir loved roses as no other flower. The stars, whose dance is fire, delight to dance for thee. It's my host's mother, the Countess, who really expects me. Many had lost their boots, but limped on, blood-shod. She in her left hand bears a leafy quince. Tourists traveling alone are occasionally drugged & robbed. Corot began making paintings of rocks in the mid-1820s. Shot glasses disguise their wounds. Peaches do not preach. The hawk scans his wide parish with a sharp eye. I've got the daylight blues. That Quinn, he strikes me as a bit too cheerful in winter, observed Chandler. Adorable Toughie prefers Saturday afternoon mass. Dance or dense? Adhesive or aggressive? Internal organs were mummified separately from the body. Jill's hometown was beset by excessive carburation. The Apache, we are told, could hunt duck with the best of them. Not drunk, but dank. Not sentence, but ceaseless. I've had enough of her lies, Tina protested. Enough. There is nothing sentient about dinnerware. What I understood, I understand. A day for violet & vermillion, and everything of silk. Jews first arrived in India during the Sixth Century, BC. The dragon was no match for Cadmus, who slew it with one deadly stroke. What will the spider do? The teapot is missing, but there, right there, is its lid. Please, before you leave, turn out the stars.

Rhythm Section

for Barbara Shaw

So quiet
where I sit
I can hear my heart beat,
steady, for now,
as a metronome.

Listen closely:
life, right in the pocket,
taking its own sweet time.

Mine

The raven of night offers no atonement. Ben Webster was a piano player until he met Budd Johnson. Through the sun-blasted field he hobbled, his foot wrapped in a shirt. You may taste freedom, but not eat it. The lone & level sands stretch far into the distance. A short stint in Fist City. Come thou, fount of every blessing. I bought you violets for your furs. Parchment or parliament? Bungler or burglar? What comes through the front gate is not the family jewels. Interior at Collioure. His father's name was Jumping Bull. You think that's clever?, sneered Cynthia. I don't. A skilled long-bow archer can fire up to twelve arrows a minute. Yes, it was one of those zig-zag quizzes. Got traction?, inquired Jake. The Hunkpapa were breaking camp to follow the herd when 50 Crow warriors attacked suddenly. Mumford acknowledged Dreiser's power & reach. She is all blossom. She is all flame. The balanced throwing knife also cuts. Not flash, but flesh. Not transmit, but transmute. Some have more snap than others. The shadow? The shadow is all right. Mir zaynen do. Just the facts. And pass the bucket. I never said mine was the only way.

The Runners

they come out of the turn onto
the straightaway—one, two, then a pack

faces lacquered with sweat
short, even strides

feet barely touching
ground, gliding toward a distance

always just beyond
now

Sugar

Hawks in flight emit a whistling noise. I have my rages, explained Baron Trangent, & my outrageous. Now is the strong prayer folded in thine arms. The leaf roll virus affects most of the world's vineyards. Some 260 letters survive from Van Gogh's three years in Provence. Ornette's recordings do not lend themselves to cocktail chatter. Who belongs to the gang in gangplank? Who hunts the fox in foxtrot? Coyotes in Appalachia tend to live in small family groups. The Ambassador's hair was so precisely black it looked painted on. Alone, I move toward the heart of the world. The first stars appeared like pinpricks of light & we all huddled in silence around the fire. A razor is not a metronome. A beaver is not a utensil. Dopamine is found in the limbic areas of the brain. Certainty!, Quentin exclaimed. Is that what you expected? The relationship between iron & irony is not at all tenuous. Cross or crass? Figment or fragment? I've grown tired of being looked at & implore you to stop. Earthquakes will inevitably do damage to buildings. Advance now across the Wadi Arnon. Clever rise not suds. Dawn & millions enter the expanding bubble of traffic, still dreaming of sleep. But what is a sheet of white paper, covered with ink? Locked & clocked, Sugar. Locked & clocked.

Work

My grandfather, born into a family
of blacksmiths, was led to the forge
at twelve & there he stood in the heat
& smoke, wearing a man's leather apron
& cap, learning the trade, holding his tongs
before him like some dangerous animal he had
managed to tame for the task of the moment.
He told me all this in a soft but steady voice
while sitting in his chair, the overstuffed club chair
set in a corner, its arms draped with doilies
faded to beige with time & wear.
He had never said much about his life
in the Old Country, a land so lost to memory
its only remaining inhabitants were ghosts,
during a century either forgotten or thought
irrelevant by most of the living.
By then my grandfather was as old
as my imagination allowed & he no longer
worked, no longer arose each morning,
walked to the subway & rode it downtown,
all of which meant—to everyone, that is,
except me—that he was dying.
Suddenly energetic, he mentioned
he could show me his scars, the marks
left by the burning ashes that had slipped
beneath the long gloves he'd worn, & so
without ceremony he rolled up a sleeve
& after 70 years there they were still,
bits & chips of pale flesh like a random swatch
of irregularly-woven white-on-white cloth.
For a quick instant, I saw my grandfather
as a youngster again, intent on his work
at the forge, & myself standing beside him,
our faces reddened by the hot coals,
children, the both of us, & determined
to perform, as expected, the work of men.

Molotov

White Feather signals Matisse's return to realistic portraiture. Radon's radioactivity makes it easy to detect. I made them see I was a servant of the Queene, a great casique of the North. Jurgens exhibited all the subtlety of a roadside flare. Caged herons have been known to bite one another to the death. Admit it, laughed Enid. We all got stinking drunk. The pride of thy heart hath deceived thee. Who sculpts the bust in combustible? Who sings the tune in importune? Much of Bangladesh is built on mud flats. Not everyone wants to understand string theory. Sets bet frost. Three gives birth to all things. In the shorter term, scientists look for any signs of stress. I am kindly, Lady Cantwell announced, but I must not be fatigued. The evening pauses on the road. Leafless shoots of ivy clung to the brick wall. Desmond's dry martini sound. Penance or parlance? Cheddar or chatter? How simple the act is. If only I could describe the courtesans of Venice. Dwellings constructed of bamboo are ideally suited to withstand earthquakes. There is nothing especially humorous about Tierra Del Fuego. It is said dancers do not regret their bodies. Finally, revealed Larsen, I decided to leave things as they were. Si tu me quiseres. We then learned her cat was named Valachi. You bring the cocktail. I'll bring Molotov.

Vendors

All evening long, their eyes
blurred by routine, the rose vendors
make their rounds from bar to bar
as every joint on the strip basks
like a secular heaven in its neon glow.
If lust or love should blossom
amid the jumble & crush
of bodies, they will gladly provide
just the souvenir to urge it on.

By now I recognize quite a few
& my face, for better or worse,
is familiar to most. We nod in passing
like old soldiers whose exploits
sound rehearsed. Years ago
I purchased a bunch, both red & white,
for a woman who, some months later,
declined to return my calls.

Nowadays we, the vendors
& myself, appear resigned to our roles.
They carry their blooms throughout
the streets like torches & although it
may take them hours to arrive
where I linger, I'm there as always,
patiently waiting for fortune
to illuminate the night.

Crawl

Certain historians treat Mary the Jewess as a legitimate chemist. The fields stuttered with gold under a relentless sun. Evan ran the streets. That's what he did. All told, the guild system lasted about five-hundred years. I've truly been a beast to you, Abigail, he cried. Flat characters never need reintroducing. Who isn't tormented by curves? A pickle is not a gardening tool. A cigar is not a drainpipe. Pat's busking got him as far as the next street corner. Never, boasted Brenda. And I mean never. Like blind men we grope along the wall, feeling our way. Pelicans fly low until approaching land. Jazz is an octopus, Dexter declared. Present or peasant? Caustic or cross-stitch? That bunch doesn't cotton to the accepted rules of engagement. Apples do not ask to be eaten. Tiltmeters measure how much the Earth tilts. Her secret is not to overdo it. One condom short of a condominium. The grandson of a serf, Chekhov always dressed impeccably. A very impatient work to keep the meaner sort from spoiling & stealing. We shall never forget the gravedigger's labor. A trumeau supports the lintel. She is the mirror in my hallway, the silence in my snowy field. Night's black satin shadow. Plato's dear, gorgeous nonsense. Everywhere, the land seethes with unrest. It's all so arbitrary, groused Summerville. All of it. Lordy, look at that kingsnake slither. Oh, lordy, look at that kingsnake crawl.

Bacon Lettuce & Tomato

He came into the Foremost out
of the cold, only a tweed blazer and scarf
against the weather, the neighborhood madman,
muttering to himself like a leaky tap
& avoiding everyone's glance.

He ordered a half-dozen BLTs to go
but once in the parking lot, sniffing through
greasy toast like a stray, he took just
a bite or two from each, then dumped them all
into the trash bin standing by the rear door.

And Cookie? Cookie stood there glowering,
righteously pissed, his every word
spitting fire at what he had witnessed,
the maddening waste of it all.

Leave it alone, Cookie, we barked
in our best cab driver voices.
He's a nut case, looney, always been.

Sure, he is, cried Cookie, wielding
his spatula like a pick axe, *& he's doing
his best to take me with him.*

II.

Midnight

A sharp throwing knife can serve as a survival knife. Ferdie liked his organisms bright spanking fresh. A simple matter of conviction. Really, it's all about the broth. I'd say they gravitated lightly. You need a little more carbonation in your life, Ira told her. Triangles find it impossible to two-time. The woman standing at the bar said she'd had enough of his junk, enough for a lifetime, & then fell silent, letting out a sigh. Duval used inaccuracy as a crutch. I'm asking you, What do you think? A good day for Italian shoes. Not multiple, but malleable. Not fanatic, but frantic. And now I see our lances are but straws. Nevertheless, she could silence you with a glance. Figs couldn't care less. Three boxcars filled with recovered human hair left Oswiecim for Berlin. The symptoms of influenza were well-known to Hippocrates. Lately, Notchkick has tired of doing the watusi in public. Who feeds the mole in molecular? Who walks the dog in dogma? Certain guilds occasionally admitted women. They preferred to do their petting outside the zoo. The essential ingredient in Vin Mariani was cocaine. This party needs me, bragged Grace in all seriousness. I'm its life. O'Keefe often painted at the Black Place near her home. Every time he's on the road, he wishes it were longer. Watch closely, the rainbow ends at midnight.

Twins

In the mirror, my mute double,
shadow of light, shadow of flesh,
greets me with a nod & a wave.
If I raise my finger to my cheek
he reaches toward himself
yet touches me, confirming my substance,
his existence, the spitting image
of an idea we have of ourselves.

And as he bares his teeth
for the hesitant smile prepared
for strangers introduced as friends,
I place him as the ghost twin
risen from my breath at birth,
dependent on my recognition
& my lead to help him to his feet.

Satisfied that time, a waterwheel
built of heartbeats, has not smoothed
our features into masks, we turn,
renewed, & stride away, feeling the other
has remained, watching as the fate
we carry on our backs walks away
from our past, & determined not to look.

Melody

Only listen to the voices of cedars & pines when no wind stirs. He wondered whether a sharp shard of glass suited his purpose. Gauguin transformed local color into expressive color. It's tough enough being myself, Rosalie revealed, let alone someone else. The two surviving species of tuatara are the only remaining members of their order. By 1500, English clothiers rivaled those of the Netherlands. The landlord was unable to explain the huge sprawling stain on the floor of the foyer. Hennessy sought permission to bark at will. That little twist is what's important. Not priority, but privilege. Not advance, but advantage. Zola's narrative technique in *Paris* can almost be described as cinematic. Planning to set your pants on fire?, inquired Trudy, eyeing the bucket of kerosene. Lotuses grow better in mud. A tell-tale red bulls-eye rash does not always appear. Sweeten my bleed, if you please. In Charlemagne's France, women not only wove the cloth, but often sheared the sheep as well. Resist honey mark. Grant lake grasp. Damon does have his little gestures, conceded Sheila. He much preferred his vegetables humid. I'm not nearly salty enough, complained the postman. Tousui left temple life to live under a bridge with beggars. How often I waited for you at the station, fidgeting in the cold & fog like a pack animal. And they departed from Tahath & pitched their tents at Tarah. A good night for a drive, windows down, the road slowly unwinding like a melody in a minor key.

Three Wreaths

Three blocks down, on the left,
a memorial to Junie, who loved
his Air Jordans & his three-year-old son.

And in the empty lot catty-corner
lay three makeshift wreaths
in remembrance of Proud, who in
a hurry one morning at 3:00 AM
attempted a quick cut
through the Braxton Houses
though he'd have sworn he knew better
if you'd had the chance to ask.

Hear that music? A few streets over
there's a block party set on high simmer,
the day warmer than anyone guessed.
Later, around dusk, there'll be a reading
at the opening of the Three Doves Cafe.

Three younger poets, all from out
of town, will be reading from the stuff
that got them some notice. And their MFAs.

Stranger

Red dwarfs comprise three-fourths of the stars in the known universe. Cyclo drivers are among the poorest workers in Vietnam. And there stands the Accuser, alert to our every falsehood. I'd watch out for his polarity if I were you, advised Serena. Some of them stretched on their backs with both legs shackled in irons not moveable. The astrolabe was superseded by the sextant. Bananas cannot peel themselves. You must be witty, reminded the Chair. Very, very witty. The razor's edge of an unexpected silence. The rainbow in the eastern skies promised a fair evening. A healthy skepticism need not extend to arithmetic. Garrison had never been afraid of the dark. She buttered her bread. She walked bare-foot through the city. Several hundred South American tribes have become extinct since the inception of colonization. The mudbrick structures of Mesopotamia required periodic rebuilding. Comets follow elliptical or parabolic orbits around the sun. Coke burns with almost no ash as residue. *Aguas de Marco*, he hummed to himself. *Aguas de Marco*. A watch is not a wheel. A moth is not a mallet. What to do with this pretty child? Desert soils are either light grey or brownish-grey. There exist actions for which the consequences cannot be ignored. He claimed more than a dozen tattoos, all drawn with invisible ink. The onset of iron weaponry made possible the growth of large armies. Rolling thunder in the mountains. Their eyes polished with curiosity. Exile is at any rate preferable to imprisonment. Oh, why do you even bother to think about it anymore?, Vonda snapped bitterly. I grew in those seasons like corn in the night. Sit down & eat quietly, stranger, or go somewhere else.

Punchline

for Gil Kline

The day I moved, my father,
his demeanor purposeful
as a hawk's & accustomed
to the work, showed me
& two buddies, all of us
half his age, how to get it done.

Where did you find this guy?,
they joked while taking a breather
on the front steps, a bit envious
but loose as any happy-hour crowd.

Let's get moving, urged my father,
stepping toward the 12-Footer.
I rose, but my two pals just sat there,
waiting for the punchline.

Three

Daphne was saved from Apollo's grasp by turning into a tree. The repeated use of cocaine results in impotence. No one had to encourage Ludlow to throw his weight around. Evenings, the fir trees take the fog. Rodin was first of all a modeler. Old tires can be put to a surprising number of uses. At that time grave civil disturbances broke out among the inhabitants of Tours. Vivian wanted toast. She got toast. Who sweeps up the dust in industry? Who pitches the tent in tentative? Other echoes inhabit the garden. I'll have no truck with narrative, grumbled Martinson. In the 17th century, the Church struck back against the Reformation. Steeple day lime dove sir tardy. Rahv well-understood the limitations of the New Left. You may find yourself sitting in that courtroom a long, long time. So shone the fresh young maiden amidst her servant girls. Some varieties of oranges can be grown only from grafts. Bud first walked into Minton's in 1941. The thirty-six hundred seconds in every hour. Swoop or swipe? Tunnel or toenail? Only the Evil One, Mara, rejoiced not. When the leaves turn red, orange, yellow & brown. Merely escaping insignificance was enough. Her glance insistent as a splinter. For they perished by their own madness. Saying he was heading downriver was the best lie he could muster. What occurs at night happens at night. Normally ravenous, blues will readily take both live bait & lures. I hesitate to say it's fiction, he said with uncertainty. No, it shouldn't be very hard to remember three little words.

Old Europe

Off in one corner
a small boy has turned
his head to make certain
no one sees him taking a pee

& across the piazza a crowd
of workers mills around while waiting
for the day's list of names
to be posted on the post office door.

Other than a few stray dogs
baring their teeth at each other,
nothing else is happening.

Only, somewhere off-canvas,
an angel silently weeps.

Snow

That harsh February, grave diggers were forced to use power drills to open the frozen ground. Slaves comprised one-third of the population in ancient Athens. You want to keep circling around, then keep circling around. I try to maintain my joints, Wally assured us. The heart remained in the body during mummification. Itinerant builders began calling themselves Freemasons as early as the 14th century. Horses were unknown to the Incas until the Conquistadors arrived. He does have his nuisance value, Ursula conceded. Unclean one, where are you going? Wolves can hear sounds made over a mile distant. The thrust of the Gothic arch takes the stress load off the wall. A mouth is not a match. A truck is not a trick. Story-tellers must be concerned with more than a story's outcome. Montaigne never rid himself of a certain distrust of historians. Admittedly, those Atkins boys can be fairly trapezoidal at times. Blythe was in no way prepared for yellow mustard. More than 400 species of birds use the Salton Sea as their habitat. Big horn sheep grow a new ring on their horns each year. I never said I never said that, she said. His legs were spread apart in a manner peculiar to his discourse. Who first seduced them to that foul revolt? Dogs were the first domesticated animals, followed by goats & sheep. The best Chinese bronzes limited the amount of tin to fifteen percent. But I've never felt the allure of automatic weapons. That slow, uncertain drive down Shadow Road. And shall we call her whiter than snow?

The Shed

During the first days of winter
I build a crude shed
of driftwood, mill ends,
rougher's leavings.

Knuckles skinned,
my bleeding hands soon stiffen like pegs.
The crests of frozen hills
surround my fires.

Inside I wait for the creak
of hand-hewn boards,
a shiver of blades to shear my blood.

Throughout the night
sleet weaves its icy shroud.

If I don't belong here,
nothing is telling me to leave.

Roses

The bell tower at Pisa began to lean before it was completed. I tell you, I've been vilified by lies, protested Harkness. Wearing their nonchalance like sidearms, the next generation comes surely on. Taylor's sheet music consisted of one page of tone clusters. Some kinds of kinks can never be worked out. The wrath of the people simmers darkly. A full Roman name was three-fold. Painted metal can be treated to give it the appearance of wear & age. Salvation or submission? Crisp or crux? Use four lanes, flashed the sign. LaFollette strived to give the citizenry a more direct role in government. Earthy browns & reds were brightened by golds or yellows. The temperature always drops when you leave the room. At 14, Sylvia despaired of evading the stares of the Fordham Baldies lurking on the corner. Who built the dam in damnation? Who played the part in partisan? With the exception of Cleopatra, the Ptolemies refused to speak Egyptian. Jean Renoir believed his father the most normal of men. You're funny, he told her. I'd like to be funny, too. Which species of beetle troubles you the most? And so I was rescued from the lion's mouth. As expected, Pat wrung things right. Quinces do not always add up to five. Slander begins as a barely discernible breeze. Stenciling was an inexpensive way of bringing color & pattern into a home. A problem waiting to reveal itself. A catastrophe waiting patiently to occur. Behavior, certainly, but not the sort they'd had in mind. Alas, there are no longer roses.

Lew the Barber

Lew the Barber claims
he is semi-retired; pondering
his options but all done
with cutting heads. Still,
he rummages through
dumpsters for aluminum
& whatnot, rolls his own
from a wrapper of rough-cut.

Returning home
from your daily round,
you may spy Lew crumpled
face down in the stairwell
like an old handbill,
the bright shards of a half pint
scattered like chicken feed
at his feet.

Come sunset
he will take his leisure
in a beach chair just off
the entranceway & smoothing
his graying hair with the edge
of a creased palm, hold forth
on past loves so pretty
they could tear the skin right
from your eyes while insisting
he is a genteel drunk,
a sit-down drunk, not some
stumbling-down wino who makes
the alleyway his home.

Stop to chat
& Lew, intent on recalling
your name, may proffer a swig
or two from the six-pack
of long-necks at his side,
growing silent as you raise
the bottle to your lips.

Noon

The coal miners Van Gogh preached among in Borinage remained unaware of his later calling as a painter. Josephus writes that Titus did not intend to destroy the Second Temple. I've been hip from the beginning, alleged Solly. For whatever reasons, everyone said no to turnips. The Neanderthals buried their dead with the bones of sacrificed animals. Dana has her voodoo bop look down pat. Our vast but imperfect souls. Let us now visit that pleasant country. Daguerre began making photographs of Paris in 1839. One neighbor's bedroom window is still lit at 3:00 AM. A cold beet salad is clearly better with grapefruit. Who can say what the gatekeeper believes? Spiteful as a thorn, she thought. Vicious or vicarious? Crowd or crow? Adorable Toughie requires a certain finesse. My mind was on the back-beat. One never expects to see a large fish sitting at table no matter how friendly it is. Is that your idea of fun?, Bradley persisted. The over-mantels of Elizabethan fireplaces were often decorated with plaster reliefs. Anything could be happening behind a closed door. Roethke, for example, died of a coronary occlusion when he was fifty-five. Now I climb high above the busy square. Going crazy is not what I'm about, Claudette assured us. Cleopatra sailed to Tarsus for her first meeting with Antony. The implacable horizon of the body. I beg of you, do not neglect the bad machine. Come into my night garden, coaxed Madame LeFleur. Nothing here will harm you. His discourse so weightless it could not move air. The sultry ambiguity of dawn. The naked clarity of noon.

The Line

There is nothing sentimental
about a dozen or so boxcars coupling
in the yard at midnight, the darkness
brightened by the clang & clatter
of steel on steel, rust on rust.

And the engineer?
No-nonsense as a headstone,
he stares at each gauge's red-line
like a tarot card. If anything goes wrong,
he decides with a wall-eyed shrug,
it's someone else's fault.

Necessity trumps love, always,
said a man long dead & buried
somewhere up the line.

Hawk

Once more the viewer is overwhelmed by the force of the applied paint. The Count was disliked even by those who won from him at cards. As a youth, Paul studied with Hillel's grandson Gamaliel. We should head due north of somewhere we've never been, she whispered. A plastic pink flamingo requires very little maintenance. The joy of two rivers meeting in a delta. Nearly half of Manhattan's population crowded into the slums beneath 14th Street. Car seats originally used horsehair & individually pocketed springs. I refuse to make sense after 5 o'clock, announced Natalie. Those assembled voted in favor of recycled content. A key is not a crucifix. A backpack is not an analgesic. Let us declare a lasting truce with the serpent within us. I really don't know much about fluttering, Harry confessed. Alpha particles traverse only a few centimeters of air before coming to rest. The cave drawings of Altamira date from 12,000 B.C. Shortly afterward, Felicia entered wearing her best lemon meringue. Wood lice, insisted Morris loudly, are not insects. One must accept that no two turnips are alike. Not fear, but fiend. Not flak, but flake. Caffeine may be poisonous if consumed in large doses. A loyal squire was expected to ensure an honorable funeral for the deceased knight. The Egyptians called them Hapiru. Bread without butter. Bread without salt. Bread without bread. The soul throws its own shadow. Set free, the heart is a small hawk.

Roosters

Restless by daybreak, the rooster
struts & pecks a path through
barnyard dust like a martinet.
Preening, he jabs his beak
under a glossy wing & ignores me
standing shirtless on the porch,
his squinting brain half-
considering sky, dried corn
white-feathered hens as I sputter
awake like a roadside flare.

One quick twist of my wrist
could stifle his raucous aubade
like a faucet, his puffed breast
a ripe fruit in my palm.
In a few hours, a tumescent sun
will pan-fry all who dare
move beneath it, its grease
our humid breath stolen
in the night by sleepless hens.

III.

Need

Try as I might, I couldn't think of any sins worth confessing. Bullets fired from rifles exit the barrel at speeds faster than sound. But the roads were falling into ruin & pirates troubled the seas. Does my heart sigh for you?, she mused from across the table. Both Sonny & Trane show traces of Dexter in their playing. Water manifests itself in three separate stages. The least sound counts, lectured Stevens. Excluding humans, no other predator can match the orca. The Magyars didn't adopt Christianity until the 11th century. You know Dorcas, he smiled. She still believes in fun. Under the Code Noir, slaves had the right to marry and splitting up families was forbidden. Unfortunately, nutcrackers do have their limitations. Only a certain type of fooling around is permissible at a shooting range. It was too late in the day for liver, broiled or not. Goof me a sprawler, will you? Whether Luke was Jew or Gentile is still undetermined. The gearbox also makes reverse movement possible. Alpacas were bred specifically for their fiber. It's better than cooking beans with onions & garlic. Innocent as animals before we fell. Who cares that Reese doesn't enjoy being a busboy? The rhythmic basis of be-bop is the eighth note. And their king shall go into exile, he & his princes together. Peeling an orange under a full moon. I long for the mantle of the great wanderers. Here, my old friend, you may have the arm I no longer need.

Roadside

If, exhausted by the blunt ironies
of the highway, you stop late
some afternoon at an old cemetery
laid out in a churchyard alongside
an unmarked two-lane, you may be
the only visitor walking the rows.

The caretaker, hearing the metallic thud
of the car door slamming shut,
the hurt-kitten whine of the front gate,
might stroll over for a look-see.
He's an old-timer, lanky, white-haired,
his face a bit flushed from two hours
of raking & sweeping. He will fiddle
with his pipe & give you the once-over
but he won't interfere. He's seen
his share of lone travelers drive in
to wander among the headstones,
parsing the passage of years
from the dates on the family plots.

He's learned the dead, speaking
their own enigmatic tongue,
have much to say to the living
& although he grasps more & more
of their buried lingo each passing day,
that is a conversation he will not interrupt.

Cat

Bergson believed time spent refuting other philosophies was time wasted. Ready to get your glow on?, the counterman asked Elaine. Limestone is the compressed remnants of ancient sea life. Now there's a crowbar you can use with confidence. The Assyrian victory at Nihriya effectively ended Hittite power in the region. Pity the poor wretch destroyed by slander. In 1800, one-third of the British population worked in agriculture. Her words nibble at me like fish bait. Fear made fine bed fellows. The Mercalli scale measures an earthquake's intensity. Osborne wondered whether the subjunctive had passed him by. Not custom, but ritual. Not rare, but sensitive. Like a breath of wind, Athena passed to the maiden's bed. So, Doc, he asked, what are you doing with oxygen these days? Sikhism began as a reaction against the caste system. Lest we forget, the sign read. Just one more instantaneous lapse in judgment. I'm sure I've seen you in Remington's, she said, giving him the once-over. Sweden or sweeten? Pistol or pistachio? Every anesthetic using cocaine proved quite dangerous. My unguents were always from Benares, wrote Gautama. Unlike bronze, iron weaponry could be easily mass-produced. Maureen's real talent was in posing difficult questions. Toasted garlic was her nickel. Ah, but we haven't taken Manhattan, observed Haggerty. Beset by hailstones large as lemons. Coffin flies lay their eggs in corpses. He liked sitting alone in the dark, the AC pumping on high, his mind racing. Search as you might, you'll never find the fifth paw of the cat.

Chablis

The joint is crowded as a stockyard
& the line, stretched along the counter
like a snakeskin, extends out the front door.
It's a bright Sunday afternoon in August
& this no-nonsense establishment
is the first package store just over the border
from a county where blue laws still prevail.
Clearly, I'm the youngster in this bunch,
well-schooled in minding both my Ps
and my Qs on occasions such as this.
The man ahead of me, tall, fiftyish, known
as Slim since his teens but dressed
too warmly—long pants, long sleeves—
for the weather, calls out Shabliss, some
of that French Shabliss over and over.

The counter clerk, a pale-faced
walking & talking potato sack of a man,
stops a moment & removing his glasses
rubs his eyes. He's seen quite a bit
through the years, we can guess,
& what he hasn't, he's determined to avoid.
By now three or four other customers
are shouting their wants & pointing
insistently at first one shelf & then another.
The clerk turns & without a word extends
an arm and retrieves the Chablis.

Wrench

Reuben enjoyed the fiery company of salamanders. Remembering my dreams would be too scary, admitted Myra. That smoky smudge on the horizon is a swarm of locusts. The use of horse-drawn light artillery demoralized the Mexican army. A plot requires causality. Only seven of Sophocles' plays are extant today. In traditional African cultures, music is primarily a means of communication. And yet Hemingway was bored by the nightlife of Seville. Dead soaks drew run mill. Upon entering, one is told to listen carefully. Not numbers, but statistics. Not sedition, but seduction. Wes Montgomery didn't leave Indianapolis until he was thirty-four. She could no longer imagine *fashion*. The number of good reasons for blueberries. No, No, No, ranted Norris like a spoiled child. We can't have all that pink. One should never complain too loudly about hush money. A journeyman is capable of working without supervision. The Bear Flag Rebellion began in Sonoma. Isn't there always a story? They wondered if it were the proper occasion for blinking. Adorable Toughie insists on pickles & chips. Early on, Wayne considered Melinda minimally invasive. You think that's Cubism? That's not Cubism. Yes, Ruby, just Ruby, is her name. A brief disagreement between strangers. Although Morgan much preferred alternating current. Savor the lush irony of red shoes. If I bring the monkey, will you bring the wrench?

Dog Tags

To this day I still don't know
what distemper is, but dog pounds
were, literally, hot beds of it, or so said
the vet, a careful, dispassionate look
in his eyes, when we brought our mutt,
who I'd named Starry because he was
white but not Whitey, in for a check-up.

Some days later—I soon lost count—
my mother told me she'd had him
put down & I was sad though uncertain
whether I was too old to cry or not.

Decades later, her eyes now welling up
once more, she told me she had held off
giving the vet the order quite some time,
it tore her up so badly. A week, at least,
or ten days, my mother explained softly,
fingering the bright charms dangling
from her wrist like dog tags as she spoke.

Wind

He packed the shallow chest wound with styptic powder & covered his handiwork with a Band-Aid. Everyone fully dressed?, she asked, walking toward the front door. The Dead Cat Zone maintains a free admissions policy. For a brief period, Boswell considered becoming a monk. Her anapests threatened to wander off on their own. Exactly how deadly is nightshade? Cost toe must heaven. Rebel soup leaving rack. Working quickly as soon as the snow melted, Van Gogh completed fourteen orchards in a month's time. I'm bored with the old vocabulary, complained Leslie. The encampment of Sioux along the Little Bighorn stretched more than three miles long. You can never go wrong with cheese, he was informed. Cleverness was not quite what Notchkick had in mind. Men grow cold when thou art named. In a second-story window, a teenage girl knitting an afghan. Pepys's diary was discovered among the papers he willed to Oxford. A cloistered nun could not inherit property, as she was dead to the world. They need more bottom, thought Ladwig. Bleeding profusely is no longer fashionable. Not pleasure, but pressure. Not prize, but price. The onset of the industrial system allowed for a certain amount of free time. All that loose talk resulted in little of consequence. Under tool the rarest but later. Into three rates though struck. Bowie's knife featured a blade slightly larger than those now in use. As you know, the Burberry Museum of Bottle Rocketry lacked sufficient funding. Deep within resides something small, feral & hungry. There's more to weather than the wind.

The Knack

It has been so long
since I have slept with another
all through the night, I've lost
the knack of it, & even
your singular body, if truth be told,
crowds me like a Pullman berth.

Suddenly, this bed is a box
too narrow to hold us all: you,
me, & at least a third or a fourth,
silent, shade-like presences,
invisible as dreams, who slip
between us, curling into the curves
of our bodies like house pets
no longer frightened by our scowls
as we doze like big cats after a hunt.

When you awaken, you may not
find me here beside you, but I can
promise I will be nearby, occupying
a discreet middle distance on the couch,
& our unbidden guests, predators
who roam only under the cover of dark,
will have scattered in the light.

Moonlight

Norris preferred to use words that didn't exist. What remained of the Warsaw ghetto was later deemed of no architectural value. Throughout the streets of Genoa ran a rumor that a certain Venetian captain lay in prison. I'm ready, she announced. Lord knows, I'm ready. To the east stood Kilimanjaro, its peaks topped with snow. The crackle of cicada carcasses underfoot. No one mentioned Gertrude Stein the entire day. Most breeds of domestic pigs are descended from wild boars. We finally solved a few of the more difficult knots. Planetary systems exist in almost half the stars in the Milky Way. Beachcombing remains an unlikely choice of livelihood. Never play the peacock, inscribed Washington in his commonplace book. Not shine, but sheen. Not conviction, but belief. The burden of the rose will soon fade. And then I led you by the hand to an empty cabin at the summit. Equus is derived from the Indo-European ekwo. Bialystok was originally called Bebostock. Walking the door pressure sew. Lest bridge clearly print sand. Frazier often enjoyed a good terza rima before dinner. Take care, as the Other celebrates our every weakness. Puissant is not the adjective I would use. A peach is not a proposal. A sweater is not a perfume. The herd of wildebeest fled in terror under the shadow of the bi-plane flying overhead. Alexis trocked the lornal as well as she was able. Yellow Bird arose & began dancing the Ghost Dance while the Seventh Calvary searched the tents for weapons. That wolves were flourishing was particularly telling. I promise you, I will say no more about moonlight.

Said

What does one say
to an old lover
during a chance encounter?

Whatever does pass between you,
you want to believe it matters.

It goes without saying,
whatever is said.

Dream

The bow & arrow arrived at the end of the last Ice Age. Cheap, ardent spirits were said to be the bane of the British working classes. Don't blame me, protested Professor Mondo. I'm merely curious. They hadn't had many rewarding experiences involving tunnels. The eye of the hawk dims at dusk. The Prince of Mercy occupies the twenty-sixth degree. Van Gogh returned from Arles with nine completed drawings. A dolphin is not a dance. A beetle is not a baked good. I'd find a way to handle it, suggested Hadley. Sources have Hengist defeating Vortigen in 457. Somehow the piano ended up in the pool. An arduous trek through the new Eastern Europe. Where have all the girls come from?, wondered his drunken buddy. Dryden claimed there were twelve knights, yet Scott names sixteen in all. Felicity insisted on Calvados. Nothing but Calvados would do. The Aztecs performed human sacrifice on a daily basis. I can't forget that look in your eye, Darnell crooned. The ends of the rope shall have a whipping finish. Not loss, but last. Not placate, but play-date. What art can wash his sins away? A skillful general does not load his supply wagons more than twice. Waltha kept a close eye on his anaphoras. Alecto's fiery torments never cease. Crockett vehemently opposed the Indian Removal Act of 1830. There are but five boroughs. The challenged chooses the ground; the challenger, the distance. All year long, the shofar hoards its piercing blasts. Later that morning, she suggested we go chasing tornados. It is no longer my turn to dream.

The Blues

A couple of years later
I got the letter she'd promised,
not from L.A., where the guy behind
the wheel of the Volkswagen bus said
they were headed, but Chi-town.
I haven't forgotten, she crooned,
her words like syrup on the page,
but the lack of specifics, the skimpy details
shrouded by a mist of endearments,
told me she was planning to.

I wrote back anyway,
hoping that with her flaming hair,
those eyes like cut emeralds,
some sympathetic Southside postman,
his blood rising to a high simmer
whenever he ambled down her street,
would slip my letter under her door.

We all know what happened
or didn't, next, although I will tell you
I kept that returned envelope on hand
for quite a while. I can go to Chicago,
I thought. I can ask around, knock
on doors. I can learn to play guitar
& stand on a corner, singing
those mean woman blues.

Point

Pozo's red scarf signified his allegiance to Shango. Christianized Visigoths ceded their rule of southern Gaul early in the eighth century. I'm not the slick, stylish guy people take me for, shrugged Karpanty. Bats are the only mammal capable of sustained flight. A splendid season for mutual congress. Do stars fall on Alabama? Every print came up matching those of Pork Chop Lewis. Phantom pain may also affect a paralyzed limb. Yet evergreens do know how to keep a secret. Not circumstance, but circumcision. Not imposter, but imperative. So, Alex inquired, is she syncopated enough for you? Pernick strolled down the boardwalk with five grand in hundreds stuffed into a back pocket. There's no sense in mourning the passing of doo-wop. We shall be the nourishment & the poison. The Benin Bronzes are actually brass. How many fezes, she wondered, can anyone go through in a year? Zukofsky refused to endorse Pound's economic theories. A flock of black shorn sheep strayed about their shepherd & his dog. Discourse is our most important product, confirmed the ombudsman. Oregon or oregano? Bedlam or Berlin? The Inuit consider Eskimo pejorative. In this way, we came to Ballyba. The plan is the body. Yes, the plan. And the body. Mance prefers being seated below the salt. GT is gran turismo. O is omologato. A busy day of constant rotating. Just this once, I'd like to get it right. The Nova Express no longer stops at St. Louis. Vultures may circle, but they do not point.

Locusts

for Patric Pepper

Given time, every conversation
ceases: perhaps someone has grasped
the inevitable lurking beyond

the reach of our words. Rocking gently,
our heads nodding like branches
burdened with fruit, we practice

waiting for a reply. In the fields
the locusts grind on, sharpening
the small knives they're made of.

Chimney

Sanctuaries for Amazonia's native peoples are routinely violated. Daddy's favorite direction was North by Northeast. Cassatt burned Degas' letters shortly before her death. The cocktail culture has no set agenda. He's quite canine in some respects, concluded Joanna. Fire hydrants, however, do not inspire confidence. I myself had never been sufficiently chastened. Copper & tin ores are rarely found in the same locale. Crocodiles will ingest stones in order to remain low in the water. A gentleman trims his nose & ear hairs. A gentleman does not make idle threats. I prefer to visit cute cities, she told the conductor. Mr. Groovy certainly likes his nitrous oxide. The Blackfoot dyed the soles of their moccasins black. Not forest, but forage. Not emblem, but anthem. What to do if the chess board catches fire? No, I'm not Mr. Shrimp, Lance corrected. The explosion at the Washington Arsenal took the lives of twenty-one women working there. Amberson puffed on his cigar until everyone had had enough. A chameleon's eyes can swivel like a gun turret. I was unsure exactly how to break the silence. A chisel is not a tooth. A nose is not a mallet. Prunes or prudence? Hearsay or heresy? Lila refused to wear black on any occasion. The huffers up on the hill grow testy when their glue runs dry. That bone can belong to only one animal. Bronze me, darling, coaxed Reggie. Bronze me. Perhaps a dozen swifts pinballed from window ledge to window ledge. Megaphones were the typical amplification device of the Twenties. There is still time to bring in the adhesive removers. He had only a dish of pears to keep him company. From a neighbor's chimney, the smoke rose straight & blue.

The Word

You can work, do a job,
out in the weather if you must.
Heat, cold, wet: it's all the same.

No problem, you tell the boss,
half-believing it yourself & counting on
the saying to make it so.

Come quitting time, your eyes
thirsting for sleep, you give
your drawn face a quick glance
in the mirror & say nothing.

Last you checked, no one here
was paying you by the word.

IV.

Other

Rumors persisted that Massaquoit had had him poisoned. Yet Degas grew to despise the term Impressionist. Accordingly, Lucas exhibited a dark turn of mind. How they longed to encounter the truly menacing. Current attitudes toward the Sabbath did not affect me personally. For all that, Henry VIII induced loyal & competent men to serve him. A broken spirit dries the bones. Adorable Toughie's spice is nutmeg. The three-toed sloth descends to the forest floor only to defecate. Twenty to thirty million worshippers visit Kumbh Mela during the bathing season. Ravenna or ravine? Jupiter or juniper? The burning of trees releases large amounts of carbon dioxide into the atmosphere. By evening, almost everyone was distraught over cross-pollination. French signs expand regularly. Asphalt now sounds new. Severe weather rolled through eastern Oklahoma & the euro closed slightly higher. Everyone needs more discipline, lectured Eli. Including you. It's just like jazz, but so very different. Put away yourself from crooked speech. Not marinate, but macerate. Not ruse, but rouge. Hominids are somewhat limited in their reproductive capabilities. Benedict definitely needs his ions re-calibrated, she mentioned over coffee. Someone must remember to soak the oats overnight. Squanto may have crossed the Atlantic as many as six times. These are not my teeth, grumbled Sir Roland, visibly annoyed. The important thing is to know how to handle a spray gun. Kicking a stone he never saw into the flower bed. Won't you lead me to some other river? Won't you play me some other blues?

The Names

A Jew wonders about his name.
"I'm Chaim Yankel," he declares,
extending a firm but wary hand,
but who knows who he is?

Hundreds of names, a different one
for every village, every border, every land,
all of them hard to pronounce, difficult
to spell, & each of them meaning,
in some dead tongue or another,
"Who, exactly, wants to know?"

Abraham was *Abram*; *Jacob* became *Israel*.
And me? I am *Schmuck*, *Putz*.
I'm both *Schlemazel* & *Schlemiel*.

Yet I'm also *Rashi*, also *Maimonides*.
Truly, I am the *Master of the Good Name*.

And in the street
when someone calls out
I know better than to turn around.

Fish

A full moon is not the best time to plan an escape. ART said the sign and everyone passing by stopped to read it. The accidental deaths of certain Burmese kings involved elephants. Arguing over vegetables has no place in a drawing room. No way I'm a pyromaniac, protested Lyle heatedly. The humid air thick as dampened wool. Jacob, she remarked, is sort of an atmospheric guy. Several species of zebra roam the Serengeti Plain. Newcomb refrained from using the word oligarch in casual conversation. A week of name-calling followed by a week of blood-letting. No spark results in no combustion. A whip is not a neck-tie. A skunk is not a fire-extinguisher. We talk fear too much, wrote Goethe in middle-age. The mainstays of weed control remain hand-weeding and hoeing. Huxley first passed through the door in '54. It's much more than a guessing game, you know. A gentleman never sends prank letters. A gentleman knows the difference between aggressive horseplay and assault. The ancient taboo hangs over us still. Who are you?, asked Nina. Who are you? Their new-found friends gushed over the rose bushes. In theory, sucker removal should be a simple task. And yet I knew exactly where the stain had been. Your body is like a story. Your body is like the sea. Your body is like nothing other than your body. Someone has to go up on the high iron, said Judkins, or nothing would ever get built. It is unlikely bears, pandas included, will ever qualify for citizenship. When sprayed as a mist, gasoline is quite explosive. Beneath the surface, the shadows of passing fish.

The Healer

He sits in a rocker on the porch
waiting for patients, stoic & abiding
as the cosmos, the shade
darkening his face like a veil.

His method is the laying on of hands.
It hurts here, he tells the first.
And here. Then a long silence.

Open up your heart to the wind,
the patient is told. Let it blow through you
until your bones become crystal.

That's it?, questions the man.
I ain't paying for that.

You already have, answers the healer.

By now, a crowd has formed.
The entire town—a hamlet where strangers
are unknown—is wrapped in a cocoon of pain.
Conversation is muted, although the words
miracle worker and *saint* can be heard.
It's been a tinderbox of a summer, yet today
storm clouds scent the morning breeze.

No one has forgotten how to pray.

Given

Joachim did not hesitate to jump onto a table & begin shouting. A snuff box was fashioned from one of Marengo's hoofs. The sea is hard & grey in the winter light. It doesn't mean anything, Zuckerman assured them. It's just a story. ¿Adonde se pone los capotes? I awoke to the insistent metallic pounding of a jackhammer. The British Hat Tax applied only to men's hats. And whose blind hand wishes still to memorize your face? Scraps of newspaper shuffling down the street in the breeze. In an eyeblink, the hawk vanishes. A brothel is not a ballet. A cicada is not a sentry. At the time of Lange's photograph, Florence Thompson was 32 years old with seven children to feed. Hirohito, however, accepted the terms of surrender despite the urgings of his generals. Trim the blatant day. Fourth drew canasta. The lost wax method encases the figure in a wax mold. To organize, said Lao Tan, is to destroy. A true knight guards his honor from all shame. Intoxicated by their cozy chat, Miranda lit a cigar. The Riot Act allowed the disorderly one hour to disperse. Did it matter, Cassandra, whether you were believed? Not sane, but sanitary. Not witch, but harridan. The entire operation, she surmised, was less than jake. I've become so cynical about summer, declared the cashier. A man of Sung did business in silk hats. Freedom is not the product of every climate. Waltz, naughty nymph, for quick jigs vex. Whatever we are given, it is never the moon.

Cancer Ward #2

Blanketed to the neck,
his eyes glazed with pain,
Mr. Royster clenches his face
into a fist as he struggles
to be the bearer of bad news.
They can't cut, my friend,
he hisses, snitch-like.
They tell me it's in my liver.

One bed over, Mr. Vaughn,
suddenly lively as a spring-driven toy,
cackles until he's short of breath.
Can't cut me neither, he rasps.
It's deep down inside my head,
chewing on my brain like a worm.

Nothing to add, he falls silent,
his stare empty as a mannequin's,
the air between us thick as a shroud.

In the hallway, dinner plates
clatter on their trays, the *cheep,*
cheep of tiny, metallic birds.

Mistaken

The leaf blades of certain grasses will cut human skin. Turgenev lived from hand-to-mouth until he inherited his mother's wealth. Oh, my darlings, promised Diana, do I have a stunt for you. A restless spirit holds the youthful warrior in its grasp. Fermented salmon dust is the new crack cocaine. That summer, Zeller determined to refurbish his inner loop. The forty-four sundown counties traversing Route 66. A lion's roar may travel more than five miles. Get down!, they shouted. And cover up! Normal or nominal? Climate or climax? Lawrence thought that Yeshua thought poverty & purity were one. Every ngaka owns a set of bones for divination. If you listen closely, some birds sound like slang. Apparently, there are those who prefer to sleep in airports. Who knows what cabbages are really thinking? The Great Wall ends in a jumble of mud & stone. Again, you get the same sound either way. The beef was marinated, surely, but in what I couldn't tell you. Yes, Jehovah's wide, unblinking eye. Blenheim was one of those tall guys, if you know what I mean. Every servant has a kingdom of his own. The full moon in all its bright menace. Surmise cut fin her dawning. Knit never tendered thy kind. Mortar that isn't fully compressed is more likely to crack. Two brother gods brought barley from the mountains to Sumer. Bring out the horses. You heard me: bring them all out. In the end, Lawrence believed Yeshua was mistaken.

Seawalls

Needing the cash,
I once worked some odd hours
helping out a buddy
who had contracted
to build seawalls
for a half-dozen homeowners
living along Lake Ontario.

At best the job
was jerry-rigged masonry:
a rented cement mixer
& plenty of large, flat stones
strewn about the shoreline,
steadily eroding
like overcooked pasta
as we labored to set row
after row of rock upon rock.

All we had to do
was figure out
a cheap, simple way
of holding back the sea.

Pain

The origin of the word *gin* is by no means a personal matter. Whether uncontacted peoples still exist is in dispute. Duct tape protects the trunks of young trees from disease and pests. Let's try something different, she suggested, although few meteor showers had fallen that August. Fulbright was opposed to the Bay of Pigs operation on both moral and tactical grounds. Enormous herds of bison traversed the plains between the Mississippi and the Rockies. Essentially, tearfulness is no longer an administrative policy. Not shake, but rattle. Not demolition, but demotion. Shards of ripe pumpkins littered the pool, yet none of us had brought bathing suits. The river flowing clear as light in the noonday sun. Until the practice was abolished, Kali was appeased by human sacrifice. A capable photographer didn't starve in the Old West. My hoarded prophecies contain few promises. While even an invisible being will leave footprints in the snow. Yes, language is a difficult but necessary medium. Shotguns are not pool cues. Kumquats are not eyeballs. At first he thought Deborah smelled like fresh vanilla. Confronting the bleak truths about fructose can be difficult. I've been down that selfsame road, professed the ticket agent, but rarely...rarely. For his green vegetable, Lucian chose emeralds. A fighting man was anyone between the ages of twelve and sixty entrusted with a rifle and bullets. Move toward the light, he was commanded. One-hundred standard links of chain, sixty-six feet, one-eightieth of a mile. And let us avenge those who ought be avenged. Because of my pain, wrote Sappho, long, long ago.

Little Else

The stars tonight are
small & distant as always

They will remain so
we are told
till kingdom come

A few seem to wink at us,
the chilled glint
of crystal: some private joke
perhaps, or the inside dope
of a lucid dream

Alone in ourselves
we have little else to do
but search the blue-black sky

waiting for its dark secrets
                        to unfold

Thirst

As suspected, the veiled lady had quite a story to tell. An unfamiliar roar will alert an adult lion immediately. This is what we do, Mrs. Bunce clarified, just not very well. The afternoon light shrugged its shoulders like a bored child. Diamonds & graphite are merely different configurations of carbon. And yet Chloe habitually pilfered small items from her lovers. Believe your sound, Miles urged his sidemen. The crystal adorning the mask's forehead signifies power. May the dew have its morning. May the hour have its day. The Edict of Expulsion was overturned by Cromwell in 1657. A painting is not a paddle. A bonnet is not a Bundt cake. Easley clearly owned more belt-driven excavators than necessary. My only wish was to cross the border unnoticed. Nevertheless, certain styles of architecture defy explanation. Some Jews adopted Greek names while living under the Ptolemies. A failure to thrive, was the final diagnosis. The cool night air unwinding through the trees. They hadn't considered absolute rule, but they liked the sound of it. Not atheist, but aesthete. Not avenge, but avenue. No, she couldn't tell you what she didn't know about reptiles. The feline blueprint is present in every cat, large or small. Here fierce Achilles once pitched his tent. I said the word, insisted Marlene, because that's what it is. En el fondo no soy cobarde. Her hands trembling, her pale eyes white with exhaustion. Why Surrealism? Why microbes? Why therapy? Why thirst?

The Crown

A gust of wind rises
at your back & takes your cap
with it down the street
& you have no choice but to chase
after it, your favorite cap,
a newsboy's, tweedy & broken in.

It is mid-day on a street lined
with small homes, the neighborhood
hushed in silence but for the March wind
keening through the trees
& somehow you're strangely happy
running after your cap, happy
it stays just a few yards ahead
yet easily within your reach.

In a few moments, you think,
my cap will be safely on my head
where it belongs, none the worse
for the wear & more fitting
than any dead monarch's crown.

Time

Shaw's great talent was persuading others he truly liked them. There are few recipes that call for chicken wire. Each halide reacts to light at a different speed. Today my boredom was terrible, Flaubert noted in his diary. Those in servitude always present themselves wearing masks. You may encounter a woman named Wonderful. You may do so more than once. One requires some device that is not a trick. Is that really your idea of barking?, he was asked. Marquez's father fathered seven illegitimate children. Shortly afterward, Isfahan surrendered to Tamerlane without fanfare. A Frisbee is not a flashlight. A whoopee cushion is not a wine glass. Joyce's conversational humor, it is said, depended mainly on puns. A pair of eyes like calendar entries. It is now the time for barracuda, they agreed. Honi soit qui mal y pense. No one ever thought to ask Dr. Mustard his Christian name. Plains peoples conducted trade long before the arrival of Europeans. Similarly, Severinson opted not to sell his soul that day. Not bitter, but batter. Not penetrate, but palliate. A rare bit of nonsense is often helpful. Someone must be the top-producing starch salesman. The next morning, Judith pleasantly explained what boxers do. Boil it in duck fat, suggested Hetler, & see what you get. She liked that nickname—Joey Bones—but she disliked the man. The stomachs of slaughtered animals were traditionally used to store food. No, this is not the hour to gape at spectacles. The sky the color of weathered steel. Mr. Death, he intoned while tapping his wristwatch, always knows what time it is.

The Mail

Out here
in the sticks, a letter
seems something precious,
like rose petals pressed in a book,
the moments after a cooling rain.

My garden patch is 40 by 40;
my hands, root-stained claws.
Everything ripens at once.

Your last note read
like the quick pricks
of nettles brushed in passing.
Grudges are like homemade wine
become vinegar overnight.

Fold this page
into an origami bird.
When you toss it
it may catch the breeze & flutter
after you down the path.

Think of my words
as a stolen kiss repaid.

Lioness

Pascal's illness as an infant was blamed on a witch's spell. Were you hoping for a good bounce?, Anthony inquired politely. The earliest clay pots were left out in the sun to harden. Her designs featured colorful zippers in unexpected places. The crowd reminded them of that night they spent in Reno. In his day, Essex was considered the most popular man in England. The chill winds gathered in folds. Not conned, but cornered. Not typecast, but typical. And let that be a plea for intimacy. The ceaseless demands of a pious life. Legless lizards should never be mistaken for snakes. The first headlights were lit by acetylene gas. I had no home in the dry lands, nor where the rains fell. Both Vermeer and Canaletto used the camera obscura to achieve precision. Yet not all bonds behave uniformly in such an environment. Consequently, Morton cleverly ignored the industrial finishes. A detergent is not a deterrent. A cravat is not a crevice. Pearl divers are necessarily adventurous, but also calm & focused. This circle must be perfect, he knew, or all was lost. At last, intrepid potash is on the mend. Do you wish to travel forever? All sacred drums are made from single blocks of wood. Each morning, Camille bathed in her little fibs of the night before. The stones looked as if they had been broken and then glued back together. Nevertheless, it is the lioness that brings down the food.

Tongues

Behind

the house
into the fields,
the dark air
fingers

smoothing
the ripples of a pond,
a thin
black spirit

winding toward
a great black egg,
the night bordered
on one edge by trees
that suck the star-teat
on the other

by the resonance
of our skins,
tired armies huddled for warmth.
We can hear the dogs

the clatter of broken chains.
Their howls rise from the hollows

of abandoned wells.
Miles beyond:
the curving glimmer of road

a honed cry
under the dry, arctic moon.
Speak to the night.
If it is ours

the tongues of the field
will answer,
fireflies under the skin.

Colophon

The display font for *Crooked Speech* is Canilari Pro, a postmodern typeface, designed by Patricio Truenos. Inspired by contemporary serif stylings, Canilari has a forceful and unswerving appeal that makes it perfect for both running text and high-impact titling.

The body text is set in Minion Pro, an Adobe Original designed by Robert Slimbach. Inspired by classical typefaces of the late Renaissance, Minion is a highly readable typeface, combining modern sensibilities with elegance, beauty with functionality, and versatility with old-style elements.

This book was printed by Lightning Source Incorporated in the United States of America.

CPSIA information can be obtained
at www.ICGtesting.com
Printed in the USA
FSHW011047230320
68381FS